Loving
FIONA

THE
STORY
OF A
VERY
SPECIAL
DOG

NINA B. MARINO

ILLUSTRATED BY LEE ANN B. MARINO

Loving FIONA

(THE STORY OF A VERY SPECIAL DOG)

NINA B. MARINO
ILLUSTRATIONS BY: LEE ANN B. MARINO

PUBLISHED BY:

Happiness House Books

(AN IMPRINT OF THE RIGHTEOUS PEN
PUBLICATIONS GROUP)
WWW.RIGHTEOUSPENPUBLICATIONS.COM

ISBN: 1-940197-63-5
13-Digit: 978-1-940197-63-0

Printed in the United States of America.

ABOUT THIS BOOK

THE feature star of our story, Fiona, was a Yellow Labrador Retriever who lived to be ten years and ten months old. For most, if not all of her life, Fiona lived with Cushing's Disease, sometimes called Cushing's Syndrome. In dogs, Cushing's Disease is caused by an overproduction of the steroid hormone, cortisol. This hormone helps a dog respond to stress, control his or her weight, and helps keep their blood sugar regulated. When the cortisol levels in a dog's body are too high or too low, it can cause problems.

There are three possible causes for Cushing's:

- A tumor at the base of the brain on the pituitary gland
- A tumor on the adrenal (kidney) gland
- Overuse of steroid medications.

Some dogs with Cushing's Disease are born with the abnormality and others develop it later in their lives, as a result of the tumor formations or taking too many steroid medications. The symptoms and signs of a dog with Cushing's Disease include excessive thirst, frequent urination, increased panting, increased hunger, a pot-belly appearance, frequent skin and ear infections, thinning skin, and hair loss. These signs can be symptoms of many different illnesses, so if you suspect your dog to have Cushing's Disease, it is best to have them checked by a vet. A simple blood test can confirm if this is, indeed, the cause of such symptoms.

Even if your dog has Cushing's Disease, do not despair! Dogs with Cushing's can lead long, healthy lives. There is no cure, but there are treatments available. We can testify that Cushing's Disease or not, nothing stopped Fiona, who became a long-term member of our family. It is our hope that you enjoy the world of Fiona, much as we did for over a decade. She reminds us that even though sometimes we meet others who are different, they have the power to add much to our lives.

FIONA was a Yellow Lab,
A Yellow Lab was she.
Her fur was draped in pink and white
For all the world to see!

HER fur was pink, and white, and rose,
From the top of her head to the tip of her toes!
A yellow lab she was said to be...
From a country called Britain, far across the sea.

HER legs were short and somewhat stout
Her chin was set in a great doggie pout!
Her tail was long and bushy and white,
She always appeared to be in flight.

HER eyes were large and big and round,
Her eyes were very, very, brown.
Her eyes shown very, very brightly
Whenever there was food around!

A wild and frisky puppy was she,
Biting and chewing for all to see.
Eating her way through slipper and sock,
One would think she was a sports jock!

HER father, after all, was Wigglin' Bullet, you see:
He was wild and crazy as a dog could be.
Chewing on every nook, cranny and tree;
They were father and daughter, obviously!

HE walked with a wiggle and a strut, oh, so proud!
It was just like he was talking out loud.
He was short, he was stout and oh, so white
And always appeared to be in flight.

FIONA Grace absolutely loved to eat!
She absolutely loved to chew on her feet.
She loved all food, in and out of sight;
She loved it and loved it with all of her might!

SHE loved bananas, apples, oatmeal and rice;
Pasta and watermelon were all very nice.
She'd eat all of her dog food piled to the sky;
If she could, she would fly, fly, fly!

SHE barely chewed, no matter what the meal.
She gulped and she swallowed,
All food had appeal!
She was forever waiting for the next new deal.

SHE ate off the table,
She ate off the floor.
She jumped on the counter
To find more, more, and more!

THERE were bagels
There was butter (mmm! special favorite)
There were veggies galore;
All for the taking; more, more, more!

FIONA chewed on paper and tissues galore
Her mantra was more, more, more!
She chewed on her tail with a feverish gnaw,
A big open patch remained evermore to be sore.

SHE ate nylons, paper, underwear and string,
Garbage, bugs, and just any old thing!
She licked the refrigerator, the stove and the floor;
It wasn't enough, she was always searching for more.

I made her some socks to cover those feet!
To keep her from chewing, so her feet would be neat.
They were pink they were purple and oh, so sweet;
Anything to keep her from chewing on those feet!

SHE hated those socks!
She did not want them on.
So she ran and I followed,
She wished I would be gone!

SHE fought and she struggled,
She twisted and bent;
The socks would be on;
I would win in the end!

I had to protect her,
The socks had to be on.
Without the socks on,
Her feet could be gone.

SHE loved her walks, each one was new!
She pulled and tugged in the morning dew.
She played "bite the rope" with a playful gnaw;
Biting and pulling until she could bite no more.

FIONA chased the vacuum from floor to floor,
Snapping and barking at whatever it was she saw.
In and out of all the rooms
Snapping and barking; zoom, zoom, zoom!

SHE loved to play with her raggedy sock toy.
I made it for her; it was easy to destroy.
She pulled it, she chewed it, she shook it galore
Working until the stuffing was all over the floor!

THE stuffing was strewn all over the place,
In and out all the rooms, in every available space.
She was one happy dog with a big smile on her face;
Her task now complete, she could slow down her pace.

SHE loved to have her belly rubbed,
It was quite a sight to see.
On her back all fours legs in the air,
Wiggling and jiggling with grunts of glee!

SHE loved to have her picture taken,
A "photo ham" was she!
She would always strike a special pose
Knowing all the world would see.

SHE seemed to know her Facebook friends
Were waiting for her pose!
There were many waiting just to see her,
As pretty as a rose.

WE spent hours in the kitchen,
Just Fiona and me.
I talked and she listened;
I told her of my history.

I spoke of cooking and family,
Of all the years gone by.
She always listened;
She never questioned why.

SHE was my friend, unconditionally.
I was so lucky, you see,
To have a friend
Who always listened to me.

SHE spoke not in a whisper,
She spoke loud and clear;
She let you know what she needed
Without any fear.

SHE would speak for her needs:
Food, water, and all.
We always knew what she needed;
We could hear her when she called.

WE loved when she spoke
In her own special way;
A delightful, wonderful sound
To hear what she had to say!

SHE had her favorite spots, you see
The places where she would always be
Where she could rest peacefully,
To sleep and snore gleefully.

SHE especially loved
The legs of all chairs.
She would wind herself around
Until her head was laying up in the air!

ONE day she got stuck!
We could not get her free.
What a dilemma it was, oh golly gee!
How would we set her free?

A little butter was in order, you see:
What else could we do to set her free?
We rubbed and we smoothed it
'Til she slithered right through it!

HER favorite chair was an old blue stuffer
It was old, it was big it was fluffy and tufted.
Just made for a dog
With a need to be stuffed!

SHE slept peacefully on the arm of the chair
Snoring and purring never having a care.
It was heaven wrapped in the color of blue:
What a wonderful sight for me and for you!

WE searched high, we searched low.
Why was she so willy-nilly?
Her behavior, it seemed,
Was way beyond silly.

THE vet never focused on what he was told;
His only concern that she fit into a mold.
The mold was that she be skinny and trim;
It seemed to be all that was important to him.

HE ignored all the signs,
All the symptoms within.
He would not open his mind,
He would not let us in.

SHE continued to act in a crazy, frustrated manner.
We still searched for answers while she ate a banana.
We learned certain foods helped lighten her mood;
After all, it was food, food, food!

SHE never refused what she was given to eat,
So we lived day-to-day, giving her healthy treats.
They were filled with eggs, carrots, pumpkin and rice.
Every morsel was healthy, every flavor was nice.

AND then one day she suddenly changed.
It came on so quickly, it was way out of range.
She began drinking up water 'till her stomach looked fat.
She could barely walk, so she only sat.

SHE drank and she drank,
and she drank and she drank.
She drank enough water
To fill up a tank.

WHAT was going on?
Something was wrong.
A cry for help
Became very strong.

WENT to the doctor and the doctor said,
"Stop feeding her so much; give her less food instead!"
They didn't listen to her symptoms and signs
Over and over, they paid absolutely no mind.

THEIR minds were shut tight with a lock and a key.
They would only speak of her weight to me.
The signs were all there right up front to see,
How could they miss what was so obvious to me?

NO one picked up on all of our fears.
All the signs had been there for many years.
Years of guessing and wondering why,
She always seemed ready to fly, fly, fly.

WE searched and we searched
Until the answers were found:
All of her symptoms
In the answers abound.

SHE was not angry or aggressive, you see:
She was not fat or eating endlessly.
Her body was hiding her illness so well.
It appeared no one was looking to tell.

SHE fought and she struggled,
The illness took hold.
She was brave, she was strong;
The illness took its toll.

SHE had an illness she just could not fight.
She tried and she tried with all of her might!
We carried her through to the very end,
Loving and caring for our very special friend.

FIONA was a special dog,
A special dog was she.
She is forever in our hearts,
For all the world to see!

SHE was our girl, our "FiFi Grace"
A friend for all to see:
She lived life through her illness,
Striving always to be free.

SHE rests now in heaven,
All peaceful and sweet.
There is no longer any reason
To chew on her feet.

SHE is calm, she is happy
Her spirit filled with song.
Smiling and laughing,
All the day long.

WE love you and miss you!

FIONA GRACE (2009-2019)

ABOUT THE AUTHOR

NINA B. MARINO, affectionately known throughout Fiona's life as "Fiona's grandma," was involved in the nursing profession for over 40 years and in legal nurse consulting for over 20 years. Nina has loved the written word for a long time, especially reading and sharing books with children. Her work with children has spanned as a mother, grandmother, school nurse, and childhood educator for well over 60 years.

Nina is author of three other children's books: *Gideon – A Yellow Lab: A Love Story*, *Fruit of the Spirit: God's Code For Living*, and *Peter and the Lemon Meringue Pie*. She loves crafting and cooking, and, of course, pets and pet ownership. In her crafting work, she is a designer for Rose of Sharon Creations.

Nina also works and operates in Christian ministry. Within the Kingdom of God, Nina functions as a prophet and intercessor. She is an original founding member of Sanctuary International Fellowship Tabernacle (SIFT), first in Raleigh, and now in Charlotte, North Carolina, where she serves as an elder. To learn more about Nina, visit www.roseofsharoncreations.com.

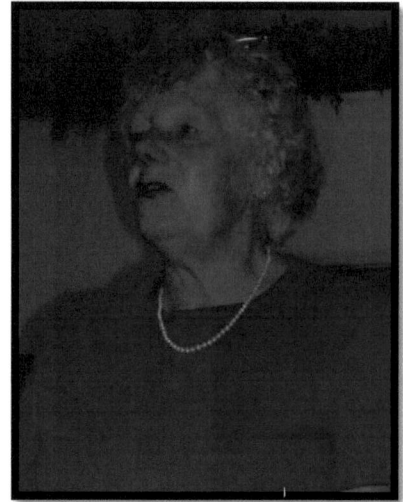

ABOUT THE ILLUSTRATOR

LEE ANN B. MARINO, also known throughout her life as "Fiona's mom," is a full-time minister, author, professor, editor, and publisher. She is author of over 35 books and has been involved with Christian ministry for over 25 years. She serves as a licensed and ordained minister of the Gospel, serving in her own ministry, Sanctuary Apostolic Fellowship Empowerment (SAFE) Ministries. She is also founder and Overseer of Sanctuary International Fellowship Tabernacle (SIFT), first in Raleigh, and now in Charlotte, North Carolina, and The Sanctuary Network. Within the Kingdom of God, Lee Ann serves in the Ephesians 4:11 ministry office of apostle. She is host of the *Kingdom Now* podcast and also serves as Chancellor for Apostolic Covenant Theological Seminary (ACTS).

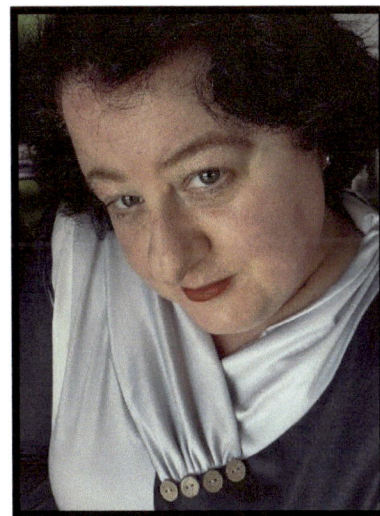

Lee Ann is honored to celebrate the life of her dog, Fiona, in this children's book by providing all the photographs, converted to painting-like illustrations, throughout this work. She loves pets and pet ownership, crafting, and sewing. In her crafting work, she is a designer for Rose of Sharon Creations and in her publishing work, Editor-in-Chief for Righteous Pen Publications. To learn more about Lee Ann, visit www.kingdompowernow.org.

www.ingramcontent.com/pod-product-compliance
Lightning Source LLC
Chambersburg PA
CBHW041549040426

42447CB00002B/107